The Garden End

Peter Jones

The Garden End

SELECTED POEMS

BLACK SWAN BOOKS

First edition

Published by

BLACK SWAN BOOKS LTD.
P. O. BOX 327
REDDING RIDGE, CT 06876

ISBN 0-933806-09-4

Contents

SIEGE

Useless to feud
against such dazzling lies.

The sham sun tempts
its own flower to destruction
burning that subservient eye;

a plague-wind rakes the path
offering seed to strangers
in the summer-house.

The garden will give way
eventually·

centuries of fountains suffocate
and the pond go begging for stars.

ASHES

Ashes in the mouth,
and the riches of the dandelion
still fall in a mist of unblown wishes.
No storm to shatter things,
to shake the mirror clear.

No matter!
Vanity falls from me
because you are not here.

ON UNCOVERING A SKELETON

There is private disquiet
in the hollow ruins
of death's anatomy—

a plangent immobility
susceptible to kindness
that makes one rather blunder
into martyrdom, than face dark
enfilading corridors—

a static tranquillity
in such carelessness of bones
put aside from all visionary traffic—
waiting to flower in the light.

CEMETERY

I should have torn his heart out
long ago, if only with intellectual zeal.

Every Sunday he comes
to scrub a small stone white
and learns nothing from his grief.

That brute cosmography
of marble and plastic flowers
omits the sun striking birch-bark
to strip the bone gently
always quickening death
with fertile trash.

There can be only theoretical compassion
on that strange island of a graveyard
where, with such regularity,
death is stoned.

RECESSIONAL

Always is time for recessional
Where yews column still parades
And a host of bland witness
Crowds the verge: scents of a fixed
Autumn drift urns crammed with stone
To relics of no exorable end; while some
Lie in wait—overlooked
By the veteran angel at the gate.

THE FALL

Scent of fresh may
hovers
before the petal carpet
is down

drifts
before the soft snow
of late spring.

Even the garden
knew
and comforted
Adam.

RITE

In China they stood stones
to figure the god of T'ai-shan
at small alleys, and prayed him
frighten the demon. He fled

or laughed. It didn't matter—
such rituals are subjective,
whether by ringing of bells,
thurification or penance.

But this burning of fields
in September is no vain cremation
of summer's last warm night.
It fires and sparks a sowing

with regattas of flame
that will defy the sprinkling
of waters. This burning wake
marks the years' future.

STREAM

The first day of sun
draws up the river and threads
willows with light.
The hoof-hard path is what the day
is—patterning the sharpness
of each minute as it falls;
and the girl turns her boat to follow.
She runs the current, and I acquiesce.

DANAE

The mist of a tired year
hangs across the morning
shy of alchemy

dreaming rooks
vault a fence, green
with growth and age

            —soft touch
              no touch—

I retread the circle
in the heavy grass
until a leaf falls

between space and time
beauty and decay

and call down gold.

CHILD OF ANATHEMA

The house is beautiful
the grounds extensive;
are there not pastimes enough
to cover a clipped lawn

but she must search
a winged dimension or fall
to writing her life
in dust?

What recreation more
for such potential
atrophy? How gather from corruption
a grain of beauty?

That fearful blackness
in the eye—
those hands like twigs
smelling of decay—

what impossibility
to memorize leaves
on a dying tree!

A LAND

This is the land of the blind
or those somnambulists who dream
in unapproachable silence,
decomposing their lives in sleep.

Sometimes they raise hands
to touch or seem about to fly
like not-quite-transmigrated souls
following obscure whims.

And yet to themselves they seem
not asleep, but poachers
among the wilds of their own night,

eliminating the good vanities
with blinkered eyes, and riding
obscurity rough-shod.

Spectators stand and watch
sometimes: admiring.

FOR HERACLITUS

You cannot hold back the Spring

children must weep for the snowman
and the worm be lodged at the root

winters have passed
and the bird and the leaf
know the dry Summer.

Walk barefoot
in the white dust
and find out the bones of the earth.

STREET CORNER

Idle and childless women
stand here sometimes
to take the dreary adequacy.

They seem to laugh and chat,
but only their bodies speak—

      —forgotten Cleopatras—
             oh,
then the withering begins

and I wonder:
did they ever use their hairnets
to catch butterflies?

COLD CHILDREN

Children of a cold month
crave impossible ease

they watch the ripening fruit
and count footfalls in the grass
to charm the sudden dark

mist holds soft fire at sunset
and nothing rushes into mortality.

But frost must strike
with its cold instant
and the allure of the dusk
shatter with inevitable ice.

IN THE FORMAL GARDEN

Almost a child again
She rocks the swing; one toe-heel
Holds the tilting world. Stone leaves
Greener than ivy overtip her dry
Fountain; weeds cushion the terraces.
Only a fresh knot in the swing's old arm
Strains.
      She toes spilled marigolds,
Dropped fruit, surf of grass caught
Between neap and spring.
             Almost a child again
She swings free of wilderness; raises her head;
Casts white shoes at the sun.

      —her hands last possess
A stone geranium. Sparrows unpick the dew,
Let fall a jewel.

STREET

Out of the moth wings the hoof
sounds harsh: and moss on walls
takes flying Lady's Bedstraw
to unbanished grace, that drifts
and falls to win the daughters of air
with gifts.
                   Growing things
have place in a country town: more
than the proliferation of dolphins
in the cold belvedere of a lord.

His vision of a mosaic floor
supports only the paraphernalia
of elegance; while this street holds
its lively confusion, conceived
in the order of anticipatory sorrow.

THE BUILDING SITE

The crevice in the old tree-root
is dark
and darker

and the silence is spaced
between islands of hard sound
left by the builders:

fire burns blue
and plays the wind round corners;
feet begin to echo
where the quietness lay.

Six paces to the edge
the cutting angle
between brick and brick

no moss on the asphalt,
no more silences.
And the smoke will die with the fire.

THE INVALID

Wheel the chair onto the lawn
while I fill her room with fresh lilac.

Silent under the maytree
she will watch incessant nature
submit blown petals to the onrush of mid-spring.

Leave her there
with her feet among the daisies
her mind running the branches of the trees
that when she returns to her room
she may cease her childlike innocence
and see the wind.

OLD MAN WALKING

He treads familiar paths continually,
disturbing little.
                    Ample time.
Ample time. They told him.

Night-walk insects weave a thread-path
flashing like trout on the eye; and streams
deep with late sunlight open his head
to fugal persuasions of doubt,
compelling as dreams.

He has maintained too long
abstinence of day, and now
is tethered to sleep.

MISS BRYANT AT THE SEASIDE CAFÉ

Coming events count their shadows
as she counts paving stones,
pink and grey; and is weary of being
a dragonfly held on thin-veined dreams.
She takes toast—with cherries;
coffee and champagne . . .
The tide is low, but she knows
she will be back when the sea
is at the window, to sip
tea—with chartreuse; cakes
à la bolognaise . . .
Fish are laid out on the promenade
with—or without—bones; fresh
from fighting gulls on a grey sea.
Here at least there is a violin.
But eyes haunt and are haunted,
as spiders decorate walls
dark as a garden end; and she knows
she thinks what she is doomed to miss.

HALF WAY

One must get used to not
returning; to temporizing
in the sudden lusts of age;
and arrange oneself—disguise
thought with requirement of rest.
It is a torpor that settles in
insensibility; and makes the bird
unaware of its song, the man
in the garden hear only noises.

GARDEN LADY

By watching, she extends her given days
in the quiet of the summer-house. Walking
is beyond her age, but she measured out
a path in earlier years, untouched now
by the prodigality of high summer. And she watches.

What's new in the breeze today?—
                                                    So
she prolongs, making no pastime
of mock-sorrow; to breathe on
but not clear the crystal.
An east wind touches the roses; she looks beyond
to the shallow stream. Too much
thought of the past
would cost her extreme litany.

LIGHT

swarms
at the gate edge
soundless shingle
tufts of sun-bright hands

the tide is full
and hangs on thistles
dead blown
empty.

Moon
confused and mysterious wine-pourer
draw away now the sharp fingers
soften the light-scarred willow

and let the day go.

BUTTERCUPS

Such meditations
of the yellow sun in the grass—

so many dawns in the field.

All midsummer
in one flower—

and so much gold!

REFLECTIONS

A willing silence haloes objects
And persons alike; they are
Neither here nor there,
But float in unprovable solidity.
Theirs is no necessary embodiment.
They rest, gazing out, in their complacency
Convinced that the property of mirrors
Frames only a partial truth.

JASMINE

Lady,
hold that spray of jasmine
with care.

Outside, children
going home through thickening mist
look so old suddenly
breathless
untidy premonitions of age;

already forgetting the sun
they stamp the ground
restless for change.

But that jasmine
is a still fountain
perpetual form—

hold it with care,
Lady.

CITY-THOUGHT

by an open window
in a closed city
the mind is contained
in one bright geranium

quick
      still

night
and the garden
holds scents to itself
until the boy comes
with the newspapers
and his dog sniffs the roots
of the flowering cherry

MOON

What passed
between the moon and me,
do not ask.

After days of hot-winged butterflies
and feet in the white dust
of villages and paths leading
to the sun's eye—
to be among silver houses
in a quiet street of no lights
but that one great moon . . .
do not ask;
                              but know
the rounded cave of cool desire
to enter and clarify the day.

REMEMBERING MY BROTHERS ON
A MOONLIT NIGHT

from the Chinese of Tu Fu

No one goes travelling at the sound of the war-drum;
Only a wild-bird cry crosses the frontier.
At night-time now the dew will always be white,
And this same autumn moon shine on my home.
My brothers are wanderers too,
And I can ask nowhere if they live or are dead.
Letters may never reach.
With new wars, to hope is out of the question.

REGENT'S PARK: LONDON

Dawn
and the sky lifts slowly:
so many birds on the pond
so many thoughts to feed

only a child runs forward
scattering the thoughts
with broken bread—

birds smother him—

To be so weary of the attempt
so ready to yield to the fear!

FROM THE BEAUCHAMP TOWER
IN THE TOWER OF LONDON

Too many names
imprisoned here

clusters of patient signatures
time-centred scrawls of death.

Below, people group
to hear a collective thought

and wing-clipped ravens
study the blown leaves.

Only pigeons ease the air free
to soften the hard stone

and a ship's siren
haunts its way out to the large sea.

NOTHING

seems to explain
the look

that passes
between man

and bird
eye to eye

at the field's
edge.

OCTOBER

walks
the full weight
of her pregnancy

searching
for last year's child
among the golden trash
of the garden.

WINTER ASH

After tea
the fire-glow: other patients
asleep. He did not ask to draw
the curtain or his wing-chair
to be turned away—the glass door
his eye. Let burning logs fill the garden.

Snatches of peace in the sudden bird
that curves out of vision.

Time
for rooks to gather autumn
in their wings and fly low.
Late-leaf bonfires tilt haloes
to placate the gods of winter.

Tomorrow the mind
again—bare in a four-square room
frosted like a cold step. They will probe
thoughts of a thin skull.

But now the garden: and nothing
stirs under the orange sky
but the smoke. Imperceptibly
the decay spreads: mortality
hangs in the rafters.
                    They will try to obstruct—
to blur the prospect of the long-dying rose
whose petals, weaker than the air that lifts them,
have journeyed generations of quiet
to be here in fragile perfection.

The garden conspires
to let nothing end.

The fire falls into itself.
Ash and leaves already lift
on a crescent wind.

Patients are waking:
time to draw the curtain
for today.

OLD WOMAN AT HOME

She wanted to stay
out in the air:

men cutting crinolined willows
to wrinkled stumps
for cows to look at—no wind:
no wild grief of branches.

She turned to the low sun
and she heard
a dialogue of angels—starlings
like locusts.

A nurse on white stilts
across the lawn: time to announce
a headache.

They went in together
and the house slowly rolled
darkness into neat blinds
and drew them down tight.

CHILD

Son of too many mothers,
you do not know such confluence
of love bears down upon
a crystal dimension
to break it, or disperse
with a cloud's indispensible caprice.

Be fugitive!
Those roots suck
melancholy: and as you comb
each other's fine bright hair, let no fancy
take the craft of poison.

TRUTH

Tonight
I bowed my head
in reverence
to the moon
and began to trace
with my feet
the patterns of tree shadow
on the path.

First
jumping
in the light spaces
avoiding the branches,

then
tip-toeing
down the fine tracery
through the veins
to the heart

until
I met the trunk

head-on!

DECEPTION

It's the casual deceit that destroys
So delicately—the warmth
That brings out the fine butterfly
In the winter sick-room to beat
Its life on an embroidered comforter.

PANELLED BEDROOMS

There are chandeliers,
haloes of morning extravagance,
cut-glass fire.

But such facts of lucidity are baffling
when old men in their beds call for light;
the volume of sun seems inaccessible
and daily gestures mere chatter
among all that passion of want.

Desire turned to silence
too soon yields a mouth without lips.

ELDERLY SISTERS

They walk quiet rooms
touching this and that
so delicately: not noticing
the sea still in their hair.

Terrified of some clouded
journey—caught between
a memory and a decision
they do not think they dream.

They arrange this and that,
their lives, so neatly
that each thought dies
unattended, that the shell

may not disturb the configuration
of days. Breathe gently
on their beauty: the slightest
passion will prove carnage.

BALLAD OF THE ARMY CARTS

from the Chinese of Tu Fu

The carts rattle;
Horses keep neighing
And the conscripts go by
Each with bow and arrows at his waist.
Fathers and mothers, wives and children
Run to see them off. Dust clouds the Hsien-yang Bridge.
They tug the soldiers; stamp; they delay them with crying.
The sound of their weeping touches the sky.

A passer-by questions;
They only say:
            'There's always conscription!

'Some of us were sent north at fifteen
To guard the Yellow River;
And now, reaching forty, we're posted west!
When we left we were too young to tie our own head-cloths;
We come back white-haired, and are sent to the frontier
Where garrisons stream blood for an ocean.
And still the Emperor's dreams expand!

'Perhaps, sir,
        you haven't heard
That east of the mountains
Brambles grow thick in the thousand villages.
Even where a wife is strong enough to drive a plough
Crops invade each other, weeds run riot.
The men from Ch'in are the worst hit—
Best soldiers driven like chickens or dogs.

'Sir,
     though you kindly inquire,
Conscripts dare not complain.
Take this winter—they are not yet
Demobbing the men of Kuan-hsi!
District Officers demand land-tax,
But where is the land-tax to come from?

'To be sure,
          it's a curse to give birth to sons,
A blessing to have a daughter.
A daughter you can marry off,
But a son is born to lie lost under a hundred grasses.

'Perhaps, sir,
          you haven't seen
Strewn along the Kokonor shore
Bones bleached long ago.
New ghosts moan, old ghosts weep,
And the sky drips through their thin crying.'

ABSENCE

Hands form a turning
world of leaves, foliage
of the body caught
in a summer storm.

A cage of fingers
tried to hold the moon
shaking light on a
familiar beach:

but still September
currents pull stubborn
bronze, and take the light
far out to sea.

PRESENCE

Every night an autumn,
a shedding of last protections,
deep forests open to possible wounds of winter.

Love rides the decaying woods
until the inevitable warmth—
and occasionally a nine-month spring.

EARLY FROST

The widow
has only
morning dew

to offer.
She dabs a
pink powder

under her
eyes and waits
all desire

to end; as
she brushes
away frost

in the first
godless month
that is hers.

THE CORN POPPY

did not
fall
to the axe
     hard with
     war-blood

but waited
the scythe

and flew
too near
the full
     to be
     forgotten

JULIETTE

Inadequate mirrors
are held—

she is
empty-eyed.

Her mind
coiled
and recoiled
in a somersault
out of the ephemeral
into the closed trance
of catalepsy.

A flower
is placed by her bed
and the clock
wound daily.

Paltry essentials
crowd the room

but her mind
has dead-locked time:
the sky still summers her days
and the rose is immortal.

A FAR DEATH

He died: you left
for a distant funeral
as suddenly as he.

And all the time the drumming
of the runway that lifted your flight—
tarmac that is a simple homing line
among so many dreams that go
knocking at each other's door.

So much fog in the trees;
death in every bright day.

LOSS

There is no rivalling the dead:

Fragments, reminders, startle
To trivial infinities.
The fabric of duplicity frays,
And comfort begins in devotion.

Is there no possible loss?
Dreams visit, and shadows walk
The stair. These shards scrape vanity,
Let grow the sweet indulgence of constancy.

ROOM

a
　self-created tomb
　　　with only
　a rectangle
　of light
　　　to separate each dream

a
　ray that wanders de-
　　　liberate
　and slow leaving
　no stain
　　　apart from memory

LAMENTING A YOUNG PRINCE

from the Chinese of Tu Fu

Hooded crows from the high walls of Ch'ang-an
Flew by night over the Gate of Autumn cawing;
And on to peck at great roofs
With warnings to high ministers beneath
To flee the rebel savages. Golden whips snapped,
Horse after horse sank exhausted;
While many of the Emperor's Own Blood
Found no escape.

With a nephrite jewel at his waist
And ornaments of blue coral,
A Prince weeps at the cross-roads.
He will not tell his name—only his despair;
And kneels to be my slave.
Already like a holed rat he has grovelled
A hundred days under thorns,
And his body is torn, his fair skin shredded.
But Dragon Seed are not as other men are:
Heirs of Kao-tsu bear imperial features.

Jackals and Wolves waste the city
While the Dragon haunts the wilds.

'You must, Prince, conceal
Your thousand-valued person.

'For you I pause—
We dare speak a moment only.
Last night an east wind brought the smell of blood,
And camels of the plunderers swarmed the fallen city.
The veterans of Shuo-fang were always upright men.
Bold in their time: how foolish they seem now!

'I hear the Son of Heaven already is uncrowned;
But his Sacred Virtue has charmed the Uighur khan.
He and his warriors slashed their faces
And vowed to expiate the shame.
But be discreet—there are informers.
I weep for you Prince. Be wary.
I pray the spirits of fortune from the Five Imperial Tombs,
Wherever you may go, watch over you.

DAWN VISIT

for B. G. G.

It was like it the day he died
—a total exile from grandeur—
unable to steady the tide
of wind in the birch, fix the hour
of the gull swinging the promontory.
Ramshackle words were stammered
through frost; the window raised
to admit a cry. And then
the rubbing of hands
against the cold—
                —and you came
knocking out of my dream
to remind me.

THOUGHTS WRITTEN WHILE
TRAVELLING BY NIGHT

from the Chinese of Tu Fu

There is a faint wind through fine grass
And the tall mast points a lonely night.
Stars hang on the level vastness of the plain
And the moon skims the great river's flow.
My writing earns me no fame;
Age and ill-health strike out my future.
What do I resemble drifting so?
A lone seagull between earth and sky.

DESERT PEOPLE: TINEGHIR

Sun tears out darkness
scatters it across the dust

and hope
taken from the desert
is nailed in hard shadow
to these layered folds
of a broken world
ruins of unbuilt cities

and the tribe falls
prostrate
before an impending crown
of barbed rock bowled in fire
before dark
and a further quittance at dawn
in the still flower of frost.

ROCKS AT RABAT

There is the perpetual window
and here my hands:

like caged birds
they search the flatness
trying to escape or find
the pulse of those dark veins—
torn filigree of rocks:

but the hard hour of afternoon
falls among the litter of paper gulls
that fleck the waves
and I am safe

untouched
in a glassy world
as it begins its callous to and fro
between the fortress
and those bloodless hands of the sea.

MEDERSA

A white cell
cut square for silence
and a sharp light that opens
the sound of roof-birds.

No Koranic scholars
but winged quadrupeds
heraldic eagles
hold the faith of four centuries
in a bowl of water
between the prayer-room and the pool
stirring reflections of mosaics
and the hanging pearls of wood.

DESERT GOD

Immensity of sand
with no flower-wound

no weathered mother
to forerun his birth:

simply a fire
that races horizons

granting sudden sight
or cursing with gradual blindness

if perpetual obeisance fail.

VAN GOGH IN ARLES

Torn earth
breaks almond blossom.

Two years
of sun-thistles
in a frenzy of burning
exaggeration

until hamstrung by resonance
the high yellow note
burst in a single pistol shot.

'CRUEL BEHOLD MY HEAVY ENDING'

Goodnight is Queen Mary's death:
a lute that bore her heavy end
through city-prisoning towers
and martyrs' candles.

Without her father's desperate gaiety
she clung to confessors
and watched the ghost of a dog
flung through her window at night
ear-clipped
howling the hanging of priests.

Then the lute resolved
the tragic cadence unfulfilled
and the Queen merciful
in all matters but religion
heard the flame of Latimer's cry
and died.

STRANGER

Out of the milk-lace mist she came

and now stands as a shadow in this wood;
restless among unfamiliar branches,
not knowing the track of the hare
or where the stream lies.

Gold-dust of insect flight
travels the trees; but the threads of light
are nothing to her in this labyrinth.
She does not see the possible eye of the wood—
its infinity of compassion
that yearns for a looking-glass.

THE LAMA

The sound
of snow-water
in his mother hills
grows flower-like to remind him
to tie a stone to his wings
and come down
through the black
and white bars of time;
to see the fisherman
with a smile like a gentle
form of despair;
and contemplate the incredible
paradox of the peace
and the hook.

BALLAD OF LOVELY WOMEN

from the Chinese of Tu Fu

On the third day of the third month
There is new weather for the Feast
And many beautiful women by the waterside
In Ch'ang-an—
Such refinement and delicate skin!
Silk patterns on the late-spring day
Shine with gold-thread peacocks
And silver unicorns.
　　　But what do they wear on their heads?
Green-blue of Kingfisher falls in feathered jewels.
　　　And what at their backs?
Pearl-encrusted skirts shape their bodies tight.

And there are the kin of the Mistress
Of the Cloud-Covered Bed and the Pepper-Flowered Room—
Ladies favoured with titles of past dignity,
Kuo and Ch'in. Purple roasted camel humps rise
From green dishes, and white-scaled fish lie on crystal.
Chopsticks of rhino-horn, sated long since,
Are slow to touch more food. And the knives,
Hung with tiny bells, slice delicate threads
To be left untouched. Eunuchs from the Imperial Kitchen
Bring again and again on winged horses
Successions of rarities.

Now with sound of flute and drum
Mournful to move gods, thronged with followers,
Comes the all-powerful Protector Yang. Shameless
He rides to the pavilion and takes his place
On the patterned carpet.

Yang-down of willow
Falls to cover the white water-weed.
A blue-bird flies, streaming a red handkerchief.
The Protector's power is fire;
Beware of touching his anger.

PERSEPHONE

Long hair
touches the room she moves in
combing
always combing out flowers:
leaf-shadows possess pale dreams
of the sun
for she knows
the lute sang in the dark
                    only once
and weeps for the pomegranate—

She, the scapegoat of seed-myth.

LEDA

Flurry of swan's down
in broken stream-waves' delirium—

you should not have dreamed
as you lay with Tyndarus' rocky kingdom

of piled cumulus
in a stormy summer.

IOCASTE

Such passionate guilt
could never survive—

taking her child of Luck
to bed.

Yet why should anyone fear
in a world of fate and the unforeseen?

Who knows who wove the cord
hanging to purify the place?

A willed silence
in the bedroom,

the golden brooch ready
for further sacrifice—

if ever the coming time were known
the next full moon would be terrible.

IN THE PARK

What to do with the salvias?

They are piled high
in the gardener's wheelbarrow
still blood-red pyramids
of too many presentiments
to go unnoticed, trundled past
the playground and the pond
where children laugh at the ducks,
and mothers scheme futures
that take no account of the stars.

THE COFFIN-MAKER

There is a coffin-maker
in the converted boathouse.

Even above the flood
of wind in the elm
across my roof
I can hear the knocking
down by the river

but I shall not know for whom
until I see the black car at the gate
and the mourners gathering
in the narrow street.

FORTUNE TELLER

Half-initiates seldom accept
those upturned images
in spite of the blazing comet
of an eye that circles the room
projecting sometimes a flickering
gallows or a man hanged
by one foot.

Such dreams are not easy

and gestures
of sceptical indifference
pointless.

The dead cards' immobility,
the palm's impassive face,
take no note of passion;

and the empty house
fills with wordless hostility.

AUGURIES

Wind strums the field—
Sounds of dry worms
That tease a bird future.
Rattling the tails of wheat
It spits at rook wings, shifts
The abacus of days.
Footsteps of a blind seer
Have trampled the gold
And all is uncertainty;
For a hellcat sphinx rides the hill
And asks where the future went—
Why was the gate left open.

PILGRIM

He looks tired
of telling beads,
hoping for hope.

Bead on bead ticks
the precise ritual
of a well-made clock
designed to reduce
the turning of stars.

He draws Orion's sword
through his prayer; and knows
no fictions in loneliness.

ALBAN BERG'S VIOLIN CONCERTO

Dem Andeken eines Engels

I don't know what she said—
that nineteen year angel who fell
into the prefigurement of his own death:

   a world before and after the struggle

'Perhaps I can live
one . . . two months more?'

It is enough.

She died:
her paralysis
became a vision of dancing
towards the irresistible catastrophe
and resolution—the arch of a violin
holding a Bach Chorale.

He too died:
in great pain, it is said,
but from his bed his arms spread
in winged delirium:
'An up-beat! An up-beat!'

Es ist genug.

His death-mask is quiet.

FOR GUSTAV MAHLER

In such a land of violent patterns
and incredible loneliness

with a childhood stifled by too much
of death and madness,

there is surely time for the Spring.
But the past pushes the incessant

bugle-call; and the future, willed in music,
offers no defence of cool detachment;

no neat-bladed crocus in the park;
simply wells of fierce integrity—

a total love of life
in spite of the broken glass of your minority.

EXPECTATION

It was so still
when the tree fell

and no one
expected it.

The village playground
was deserted
and no moon yet—
only a false sodium dawn
on the by-pass,

straight netball lines
an empty goal mouth
and a swing
pushed by the ghost of a child.

And then the tree fell;
and with it
all the stars in the universe.

The sky was empty
and no one expected it.

VICTIM

Shed the remnant of your greatness
there in the field,
where poppies
scatter their red evidence
of a bright day:

for memory
is more shrewd than life
and the dead lie still
in uncut grass.

GRASS WIDOW

At sunrise they watch her
go to the window; see
the daily gesture
of those who are alone.

Her mouth is parched
fearing the growing beauty of dreams
that parted her lips in sleep.

Sunlight on the jetty,
morning on the unspotted sea.
Every dawn she must unpick her dreams.

Five years have taught her body
the lack of life; if he does not return
how will she know the time of falling?

NECROMANCY

is no mystery
in spite of the blown seed

the moon draws
the willow-herb to fine cloud
hollyhocks to ultimate modesty

drift of dull fur
confuses birth
foretold in the wind's course

What sorcery in that?

Time must follow time:
the feathered seed
its predetermined end.

LICHEN 1968

I have been walking
the dead seeds of remembered trees
watching the wind pile them
like a mad dream
into a concentration of bones

and the smoke of bonfires
seemed to hold the sick scent of burning man.

My fingers are so long
and thin—
        pianist's fingers
cultured   fine—
as they touch the damp growth
on every trunk between here and Spring:
                        lichen
blown on the wind that carries Auschwitz still
to god knows where
and leaves green life on these sycamores
here in England
now.

MISSIONARY

Unmaimed, you come walking.

Tendrils of soft roots
crush walls in season;
here monkeys sometimes scream
and the black and rotting logs
that clutter the compound
lift bowls for water.

You raise your hands
and bring sin to the falling
in their decay.

MAN IS MOCKED

the mist has fallen
from the sun

and the trees
take on

a covering
denied the man

in his garden
planting saplings

FOR MY GRANDMOTHER WHOM I NEVER MET

Do not hammer the cloud
as death takes you from the beautiful world
for this is the deeper night
when room must be left
for the secret movements of the dark.

Lay those grey hands on greyer lips
and be silent: keep still
those thin and drowning eyes

and in this
your last hour of light
allow latitude for your dying.

SEAGARDEN FOR JULIUS

[extracts from a sequence of poems in memory of the pianist Julius
Katchen who died of cancer in spring 1969]

Sin in illusion
Guilt in truth

Sit
    by the fire
    in winter

hear
    the silence of flowers
    on the window

    the cry of ice
    in the newcut night

listen
    but do not disturb
    the cadence of cold

*

Nothing for me—
nothing of future
(I am used to tomorrow).

Take away the flying ant to come
and with him his city:
plant your foot across his path
smother his palaces
and wait to be eaten in dreams.

*

So
this is my garden
today

fragments of garden tide—
attrition and growth—
the broken shells—

The sea washes at the house
and dreams rebuild it.

*

Child and man
with the same eyes
search the horizon's hideous purring;
with the same fears
leave the cliff-top

hurry home at the first chill sound—
notes to peck off your nose,
cries that gnaw the liver.

The shadow follows
watched by a one-eyed moon,
the half-blind owl in the tree.

*

The mind discovers itself
only in dreams

declares a vision
and drinks at the moon—

a shadow and its shadow
to break with the day.

Then wing-flight
across a crazed sand shore

a tall mast
points a failing star—

but always
a certainty of waves.

*

Sea-feathers stroke
not like the sun
but drawing seven wings
towards the shore.

The holiday child
runs to and fro
weaving patterns
of footprints, laughing—

fresh morning canvas
evening absolution.

The man stands,
feels the touch of cold
and lights seven candles
to warm his soul.

*

Lord
let me know
mine end—

vain
shadow

until the tale
is told.

*

A garden
of tombs on a hill
over the town

straight flowers of stone
eaten by rain
fed by bone

caged wax in memory
and daffodils' yellow birth
in the grey city's ambiguity.

*

memory feeds
on thought

eats away
present truth

turns
to remember shadows

music lost
drowned by the past

preludes
drawn from air

by the willow-haired pianist
in a closed room

until the only thought
is memory

the only memory
sound

*

No peace on the receding shores:
no consolation among the trapped boats,
the elms creaking.

Incessant beaks
crowd the day.

The garden is closed
and the sea encloses.

The air only
is a clause of liberty.

*

'Come,
the wax
the thread
the measure of feathers
to match the wing

between nature
the midway course,
safe pass between
earth and heaven.'

The death, floating in water,
broken wings on the sea.

And a lapwing
first of its kind
mocks the garden burial
flutters close to earth
articulating the fall of man.

*

Death is quiet:

a trellis of bone fingers
obscures
the near skull

white head
alone in darkness
silent pain

only the roots stir
and stretch
shapeless

with no flowering:
dreadful crop
sown in the body

parasite
in the flesh
like a maimed child.

Sea-weed
on the ebb-tide.

NIMROD

Do not bring that flight to earth:
We have learned too much of compassion—
Too many the familiar times
To wear dry willow.
                          Nightly the drawn eye
Of the leveret haunts my sleep,
The sad deer's cry holds the morning,
And daily I enfold the neck of the swan.

Cover your arrows.
We know too well.

THE HERON

It stands on one leg
head-hunched, with no poise
of secret attraction, no eye
of mystery to hypnotize eel
or mouse.
                          Equivocal serenity,
that takes in the marsh's
complaisant track, covering
the journey to the shallows.

The heron is still
and stays so;
until plumed lightning strikes
from its endless patience.

ORPHEUS

Was it so long ago
I sprang from the light
In the full song of innocence,
Now fallen as the fissured rock
In which my torn head lies?

Oblivion breaks: exposes
The penalty of life
For playing the beast with birth,
Plucking the lyre at death.

Open me up a second time,
You women of Thrace!
Let in the dark.

MIRROR

for Garry and Nina

Nothing has gone out of my life
but the obliterating beauty

pale orchid like an embalmed saint
overlaying patterns larger than itself

to make the rock of Giotto
blossom in a stone tower.

Or a wild reminder of the East
in a powdery wing ready for summer—

antiquity
secure in fragile dust.

Nefertiti
perhaps she was the first

and the rest a mere incense
across some sacred glass.

THE HILL

No light penetrates in summer.
They gave it a name once
to fix its growth, forgetting
winter's transparency.
The name died before the hill
so they gave it another
to pin down unseen draperies
stirring like deep fish.
In spring winds blow the hill
out of its final death-place and begin
to move the vinous sleep of warm-eyed girls;
and there is deadly flippancy
in the mating of insects.
Cartographers smile in their defeat.

ALIEN

She walks sometimes the bottom of the sea
following the track of some seaworm
among blunt anemones—
anal mouths that draw in light
departing with the shallows. Heavy waters
hold her path, where currents will,
to cold crypts like arbours of hell.
Black scallops of a flowing tide
lift inspired weed—or hair—

things arrange themselves by propinquity—

I am full-blown, she cries,
and lurches deeper into dark.

SEASCAPE

Impossible to stir far
from the sea, and passion's fine sand.
There to be continually in touch
with the short-lived wave
upon wave. No fatal ambiguity
in the ebb and flow that takes
and brings certainty beyond the intermittent.
Attrition creeps the shore;
and morning after morning the sea.

UNDERTOW

The sea-bed is trapped
in its own decor; unseen fish
like birds in full willows
drift from cage
to cage of artful beauty.
And here in the shallows
there is sweetness in the simple waves
that come to sift at my feet,
and I am charmed almost into forgetting
the undercurrent, invisible
in its familiarity.

LIGHTHOUSE

All night gulls have been pirouetting,
eye to eye with the light. They focus
a dazed passion as they scream
elation or death at a point sharp as an edged rock.
The house, for a split of time, is Argus-eyed,
or a tree of festive globes—then total dark,
but for a rocky nest of bewildered gulls
and torn wings lifted from reflection.

THE POET

becomes his own symbol:
tiny
stained-glass insect

caught in the sun of his
own eye
focusing heat

of imagination's
ardour:
doomed to quiet self

immolation.

RAIN

the sound
of the rain
is foreign
after the drought

it ticks
on the roof
like the clock
by my bed

which you
always remove
before
we sleep

DREAMS

The literal sun
goes down
switching off
gnats
on the way;
turning the leap
of fish to rainbow.
The moon
begins
with owl hoot
and unseen wings.
The woman alone
sleeps a dream parturition
and smiles,
as Venus deserts
her heaven for Adonis,
and a child rides
his monster toy
to see
the Queen
at tea.

MEDITERRANEAN BEACH

Frieze
of summer youth
hastens
to die in the dark
warmth of the body

and the absurd
consequence
of such sumptuous death
is a pale wreath
of incompetent angels.

SAND

is fruit
on the shore
where figures
enclose sharp sun

kisses
to be salt
when the fruit
is gold

and ecstasy
spent
long since.

PAVANA: LACHRYMAE

Cast your shoes
from this green world
and dance in the bright dew-grass

move with joy
until the sky turns gold
and touch the ground that you may pass
like an uncursed Midas in an orchard
through tears that fall like fruit
through leaves that sing like glass

then move to your burnished bed
and await
the slow sway of the Passionate Tread
that comes with the last of the sun.

Sing, my chaffinch,
sing in this green-gold world
and forgive
as the Seaven Teares are shed.

THOUGHTS OF LI PO
FROM THE WORLD'S END

from the Chinese of Tu Fu

Cold winds rise, here at the world's end.
What word have you for me, my master?
The migrating geese, when will they come?
Autumn waters swell the lakes and rivers.
Art despises success
And those voracious demons in the mountain
                              laugh at your passing.
You should commune with the ghost of that
                              other exiled poet!
Drop verses into the river Mi-lo as an offering to him.

PAYING RESPECTS AT THE TOMB OF MARSHAL FANG

from the Chinese of Tu Fu

Far from home I draw up my horse
To take short leave of this lonely grave.
The soil is damp with recent tears
And the low sky is broken cloud.
Once I sat with the great man at play
And now can offer merely this brief token.
Departing, I see blossom falling in the woods
And the song of the oriole follows me.

NOTE

COLLECTED HERE are poems from *Rain* (1969), *Seagarden for Julius* (1970), and *The Peace & the Hook* (1972), as well as more recent work. The earliest poems date from 1967, the most recent from 1977—a decade of them. Because it seems to me that, despite changes in technique and tone, the poems follow from certain consistent impulses, I have preferred to group them thematically or to place them in abrupt juxtaposition, rather than preserve what would be an unilluminating chronology.

Reviewers of my early work labelled it 'neo-imagist', and this journalistic judgement led me to a study of the Imagists which resulted in my anthology *Imagist Poetry* (Penguin Books). This work helped me to understand and then to question Imagism, a questioning later intensified when I prepared a study of the subject for *Les Avant-Gardes Littéraires au XXe Siècle*. Imagism seemed remote from my own purposes as a writer—a term casually and inaccurately applied to poems of mine which may accidentally have suggested in subject-matter, if not in subject or organization, some similarity with a spent movement. Not that I would wish to deny the justice of Pound's 'Don'ts'—cautions that have always struck me as sensible and, for serious writers, irrefutable. But they can be accepted for other approaches and subjects than those prescribed for Imagists. They apply, Pound never tired of reminding us, to the poetry of the past as well as that of the present. They are not arbitrary commandments but lessons of an at once catholic and discriminating reading of literature. Pound directs one, I believe, beyond convention, into that more vital channel of tradition.

In the late 1960s, my study of Chinese affected my approach to organization by juxtaposition. This was a lesson more rewardingly taught by Tu Fu than by the doctrinaire Imagists—though, needless to say, the best of the Imagists outgrew doctrine. Imagism was no more (and no less) than a strict training for their later work.

The quicksand of ill-understood free verse was ready to swallow the lesser Imagists. Their fate prompted me to experiment with syllabics and rhyme—internal and conventional. A few of these experiments are included in this volume.

The reader will no doubt detect in the poems some thematic echoes of work by other writers—in the North African poems, Camus; in other poems, Pasolini. But the most important change in my approach to writing was the result of my re-reading Emily Dickinson's poems. The verbal texture of her verse, if not her rhythms, became a vital touchstone for me. It is a texture which one finds—in a different form, and used to different ends—in the work of Marianne Moore, the fusion of abstraction or deep perception of an emotional or intellectual fact with imagery—not distanced into a consistent correlative artifact, but acknowledging its subjective source; not the 'imagist' image—pure and freed of context— but the image integrated with context as fully as possible. This is a lesson one cannot learn altogether consciously, nor can even the most acute critical reading entirely exhaust its precise mystery. Nor is it a lesson these poems can claim with confidence to have learned.

BLACK SWAN BOOKS
Literary Series

- ☐ H. D., *Bid Me to Live*
- ☐ H. D., *Hedylus*
- ☐ LAWRENCE DURRELL, *The Ikons*
- ☐ D. H. LAWRENCE, *Ten Paintings*
- ☐ ADRIAN STOKES, *Unity of the Stream*
- ☐ VERNON WATKINS, *With All the Views*
- ☐ W. B. YEATS, *Byzantium* (ill.)
- ☐ MICHAEL HAMBURGER, *Variations*
- ☐ PETER WHIGHAM, *Things Common, Properly*
- ☐ PETER RUSSELL, *All for the Wolves*
- ☐ PETER JONES, *The Garden End*
- ☐ RALPH GUSTAFSON, *At the Ocean's Verge*
- ☐ EZRA POUND / JOHN THEOBALD, *Letters*